THE GENIUS OF
Womanhood

KAREN DOYLE

Library of Congress Cataloging-in-Publication Data

Doyle, Karen.
  The genius of womanhood / Karen Doyle. ~ 1st North American ed.
      p. cm.
  Originally published: Canberra, ACT, Australia : ChoiceZ Media, c2008
  Includes bibliographical references.
  ISBN 0-8198-3109-3 (pbk.)
  1. Catholic women~Prayers and devotions. 2. Women~Religious aspects~Catholic Church~
Meditations. 3. Femininity~Religious aspects~Catholic Church~Meditations. I. Title.
  BX2170.W7D69 2009
  242'.643~dc22

                                  2009012857

Original edition published in English under the title *The Genius of Womanhood* by ChoiceZ Media, Canberra ACT Australia

Text copyright © 2008, Karen Doyle

Graphic Design by Vanessa Hansby, Jeanine Doyle

Photography by Jeanine Doyle, Jonathan Doyle, Warren Marsh, Greg Power, Mary Emmanuel Alves, FSP, and istockphotot.com

Additional design on North American Edition by Rosana Usselmann

First North American Edition, 2009.

Published by Pauline Books & Media, 50 Saint Paul's Avenue, Boston, MA 02130-3491

Printed in Korea

www.pauline.org

Pauline Books & Media is the publishing house of the Daughters of St. Paul, an international congregation of women religious serving the Church with the communications media.

1 2 3 4 5 6 7 8 9   13 12 11 10 09

Dedication

This book is dedicated to the memory of my very dear friend Catherine, who lived the remaining days of her life as a gift to those she encountered.

Introduction

Our culture today is suffering from a deep crisis caused by confusion over the true meaning of femininity and womanhood. A sea of conflicting images and expectations has meant that this confusion not only affects women individually but goes right to the heart of society, affecting men and children in a profound way.

Pervading our culture we have what Pope John Paul II described as "a *culture of death*," in which human life is not valued. As guardians of the heart and protectors of life, women hold a particular key in turning this "*culture of death*" into a "*culture of life and love*."

This can only happen when women know what they have to offer. Far from being a problem, women need to know they are in fact an answer, and that those qualities that are unique to womanhood are not something of which to be ashamed but rather need to be fostered and encouraged. Pope John Paul II refers to those qualities that are unique to womanhood as the "*feminine genius*" and without them, he says, society is impoverished.

This book is a collection of thoughts and reflections on what it means to be a woman and those qualities that mark the feminine genius.

It is my hope and prayer that this book will help you to engage deeply with the meaning of your existence and your vocation in life and become part of the answer we so desperately need.

With love,

Karen

The Feminine Genius

...those qualities that are unique to womanhood...

Receptivity,

Sensitivity,

Generosity,

Maternity,

...without these qualities
humanity is impoverished.

These qualities are intimately tied to the structure of a woman's body.

"Objective realities reveal something not just biological about her inner and real form. The body is an outward expression of inner qualities."[1]

Karol Wojtyla

Woman

protector of life, guardian of the heart...

Among the many gifts that Pope John Paul II left the world was his work on the human person and how God is revealed in and through the human body. This work is commonly known as the *"Theology of the Body."* It represents a unique and powerful contribution to the Church's understanding of what it means to be a man and a woman, and how we should relate, and do so in the context of the meaning and purpose of our lives.

In seeking to understand womanhood, we must begin by examining God's original plan for the human person. It is only here that we will find the hope and answers for which we so desperately search.

Created as male and female, we are designed, right from the beginning, for union and communion. Written within ourselves, heart, mind, and body, are clues to God's original plan. Each and every human person is created with the capacity to love and to be loved, and it is, often surprisingly, in our differences that this is made both possible and fruitful.

In our relationships we are called to exist as a GIFT for one another, to make as Pope John Paul II described, a *"sincere gift of self."* It is only in this laying down of one for another that we truly come to experience genuine fulfillment and self-realization.

In a fallen world this is not always lived out. We are all too familiar with the ways in which men and women seek to undermine and violate each other; we experience unrest in relationships. What Pope John Paul II offers is the hope and belief that we can reach peace, joy, and satisfaction in our relationships through a deep and thoughtful reflection on the creation narrative in Genesis, which richly unfolds God's original plan for all creation as intended from "*the beginning.*"

Scripture reveals that *in the beginning* woman was created as man's equal. After the man had named all the creatures in existence, God recognised that it was not good for the man to be alone. In a creative moment of supreme gift and blessing, he created woman and presented her to the man and the man to her as a reciprocal GIFT, each to and for the other.

And so right from the beginning of time, man and woman are called to exist side by side in a relationship of complementarity rather than competition, to be a gift to one another.

We are designed for relationships, both with men and with women. In order to experience healthy relationships we must be at peace with our femininity and know what we have to offer. Every woman has incredible dignity, worth, and purpose simply because she has been created as God's daughter. And it is only in this light that we will discover our origin, our identity, and our destiny.

Modern society is marked by a culture of death in which human life is not valued. It is women who play a crucial role in restoring and building a culture of life and love.

"In transforming culture so that it supports life, women occupy a place, in thought and action, which is unique and decisive."[2]

John Paul II

"With closest custody, guard your heart, for in it are the soureces of life."

Proverbs 4:23

You were created
purposefully,
meticulously,
& beautifully,
to reflect something of the
divine nature of Almighty God.

"God created man in his image; in the divine image he created him; male and female he created them."

Genesis 1:27

God's Daughter...
your **origin**,
your **identity**, your
destiny...

"Your **adornment** should not be
an external one ... but rather the hidden character
of the **heart**, expressed, in the imperishable
beauty of a gentle and calm disposition,
which is **precious** in the sight of God."

1 Peter 3:3-4

The deepest cry
of a woman's
heart is
"Am I
beautiful?"
...The answer must
come from God
first. Only then
can a woman
approach a man
from a position
of inner strength
and security.

Receptivity

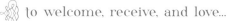 to welcome, receive, and love...

Receptivity lies at the very heart of the genius of womanhood and embodies significant implications for our destiny, role, and purpose as women. Created in the image and likeness of God, women are called to mirror this image and likeness in their own unique way, a way that is not lesser nor greater than that of men, simply different. Importantly, difference does not mean opposition.

From the beginning man and woman are created as complementary partners, and are called to image the love that exists within the Trinity in a relationship of mutual giving and receiving, what Pope John Paul II would call a *"relationship of self-donative love."* This vocation to love is inscribed in our bodies as male and female. For married couples, it finds its fullest expression in the marital relationship, in which sexual union profoundly illustrates the receptive acceptance by a woman to the invitation of love from a man.

In his encyclical *Mulieris Dignitatem: On the Dignity and Vocation of Women*, Pope John Paul II highlights this profound mystery of our existence when he comments: "The Bridegroom is the one who loves. The Bride is loved: *it is she who receives love, in order to love in return.*"[3] Scripture speaks not only of the great mystery of marriage but also the way in which this sacred relationship is a symbol that reflects the relationship between God and his people, in which the bride (the Church) receives and responds to the gift of love from the bridegroom (Christ).

It is in the receptivity of womanhood that we can provide all people, and indeed the Church herself, with an example of how one is to receive the gift of love offered by God the Father. The receptivity of womanhood is not a passive state, but rather it is an active receiving of the gift of life and love. Regardless of our actual state of life, every woman is called to this active receptivity. In order to be open to this active receptivity, our heart and mind must be receptive before God. Proverbs 4:23 advises: *"With closest custody, guard your heart, for in it are the sources of life."*

The heart of a woman is foundational to her receptive nature. Yet to risk love is to risk hurt and rejection and with that, a woman's heart may become hardened. In the complexity of our lives and following the example of Mary, we are called to say a constant "YES" to love, to risk all, and to take the journey of forgiveness in order to stay receptive before God and the people in our lives. However, this receptivity does not mean staying in abusive, violent, or exploitive situations. As women we should never betray the original dignity that we have as God's daughters.

It is this receptivity, this precious quality of the feminine genius, that is foundational to building a culture of life and love.

Far from being a passive state, the receptivity of womanhood is deeply grounded in an active yes.

In this active receiving the woman is called to a deeper gift of self, and in giving herself, she discovers herself.

Womanhood has a **particular** **uniqueness** that must be fostered and encouraged.

Sexuality is central
to receptivity.

Sexuality affects all aspects of the person...

"I adjure you, daughters of Jerusalem... Do not arouse, do not stir up love, before its own time."

Song of Songs 8:4

" '[M]asculinity' and 'femininity' are distinct, yet at the same time they complete and explain each other."[4]

John Paul II

Sensitivity

 to see the deepest needs of the heart...

The sensitivity that is so integral to the feminine personality is an ability to see and understand the deeper needs and longings of the human heart and to respond with love. This quality is intimately and profoundly connected with our ability to carry and bear new life. Regardless of whether this ability is physically fulfilled in childbirth, the very fact that our bodies are endowed with this capacity naturally predisposes our personality to be attuned to the human person in this particular way.

Pope John Paul II places enormous value on this sensitive and life-bearing quality of the feminine genius, arguing that it is vitally important that women make their contribution to society and the world. So important is it, that he believes entire cultures are impoverished by its absence.

As women, we play a crucial role in humanizing society and restoring a culture of life and love. However, this is only possible if our hearts and minds are receptive before God and we are at peace with our femininity.

For too long many women have felt that this aspect of their personhood, this innate sensitivity, is a weakness in their personality, one that limits their social equality.

Sadly, some women have been deeply hurt and so seek to deny their sensitive nature, becoming embittered toward others, hardening their hearts, and seeking to masculinize their personality. For whatever reasons this happens, society suffers when women reject their femininity in this way.

In denying the sensitive nature that is unique to womanhood, there is a loss of that which only a woman can bring into the world. When people experience a dehumanizing lack of sensitivity, a culture of death emerges where life and love are no longer the highest values and the dignity of the human person is not upheld.

Rather than being seen as something to be rejected and overcome, the sensitive nature of womanhood, filled with the grace of God, is something to be nurtured and affirmed. Far from being a problem, we face a time when we must see ourselves in the light in which we were created and realize that we are in fact an answer to so many of society's problems. Our culture desperately needs women to re-engage with this beautiful quality of womanhood, to allow our hearts to be softened by the love of God so as to be made truly sensitive to the needs of a world hungry for gentleness, love, and peace.

The moral **&** spiritual strength of a woman
is joined to her awareness that God entrusts
a human being to her in a special way.

When women embrace their feminine qualities, society flourishes.

A woman will never **discover** her true **identity** or purpose when she seeks to be like man...

She must engage on the
deepest level with her
feminine identity.
Only then will she come
to self-fulfillment.

"In the name of liberation from male 'domination,' women must not appropriate to themselves male characteristics contrary to their own feminine 'originality.' There is a well-founded fear that if they take this path, women will not 'reach fulfillment,' but instead will deform and lose what constitutes their essential richness."[5]

John Paul II

...Called to come alongside
and be helper,
companion,
friend & complementary
partner

"It is not good for the man to be alone
I will make a suitable partner for him.

Genesis 2:

In the journey of self discovery and healing, women must not forget the intrinsic value and significance of masculinity as well.

Generosity

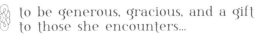 to be generous, gracious, and a gift
to those she encounters...

The qualities of receptivity and sensitivity, so foundational to the feminine genius, in turn give rise to a spirit of generosity that places value on the human person in a unique way.

By nature of design, a woman's capacity for generosity and selfless love can be truly extraordinary. This capacity for generosity is closely connected to a woman's receptive nature and is most profoundly experienced when she donates her body to a new life growing within her, but it is certainly not limited to this.

Generosity can be realized by women of all ages, all cultures, and in all states of life. But it is in the small moments of each day, when a woman would rather choose herself over another, that this quality is most powerfully developed. Far from being something that comes easily, a generous spirit requires an attentiveness to the motives of the heart and often a deliberate choice to act despite oneself. Mother Teresa often said that if we love until it hurts, then there can be no more hurt, only more love.

In Mary, the Mother of God, we see the perfect example of a generous spirit. In her saying "yes" and choosing to co-operate with God's plan for redemption, salvation was made possible for every person.

In his extraordinary work on womanhood, Pope John Paul II constantly directs women to Mary as the exemplar of how to live, how to be a disciple, for both men and women.

The tragic irony in a culture that pushes self-fulfillment through self-assertion is the failure to realize that true and lasting fulfillment can only come through a generous spirit that places the needs of others first and seeks to make a gift of oneself in love.

In Mary, we see all of the qualities of the feminine genius lived out perfectly. Rather than seeing her as an unrealistic ideal, Pope John Paul II encourages all women to pray for the grace and wisdom to live the feminine genius in all its expressions wherever they are planted, and in doing so make their own contribution to a new understanding of a true feminism that is essential for the future of civilization, a civilization of love.

True freedom & self-realization are experienced when a person seeks to make a sincere GIFT of herself in LOVE.

"The hour is coming, in fact has come, when the vocation of women is being acknowledged in its fullness, the hour in which women acquire in the world an influence, an effect, and a power never hitherto achieved.

That is why, at this moment when the human race is undergoing so deep a transformation, women imbued with a spirit of the Gospel can do so much to aid humanity in not falling."[6]

"She reaches out her hands to the poor,
and extends her arms to the needy."

Proverbs 31:20

Women can achieve great works through their yes to Go
...it was through Mary's fiat, her yes to God, that the Savior
of the world was born.

A woman makes a unique GIFT of herself through the generous donation of her body to nurture new life.

Mary is the archetype for the whole human race. In her, one sees how the bride is called to respond to the gift of love from the bridegroom.

Maternity

 by nature of design all women are
inclined toward motherhood...

Tied intimately to the female psyche, and a quality that deeply defines our genius as women, is our ability to co-operate with God in bringing new life into the world.

While some forms of feminism seek to deny the relevance of the female body in relation to a woman's role in society and the family, Pope John Paul II places enormous emphasis on the importance of the female body as revealing something of the deeper nature of our vocation in life.

One of the great joys and mysteries of the feminine genius is the capacity for motherhood, both physical and spiritual. Unlike men, as women we are endowed with a special capacity to house and nurture new life within our very body. Whether a woman goes on to bear biological children or not, it is the ability to carry life within us that profoundly shapes our personality and defines our vocation.

While it is true that a married woman and mother makes a sincere gift of herself in love, so does the single woman and the woman who commits herself to virginity for the sake of the kingdom.

Virginity and physical motherhood are the two dimensions in which the female personality can be truly fulfilled. As Pope John Paul II highlights, both of these dimensions are united in Mary the Mother of God, in an exceptional manner. In her we see how these two dimensions explain and complement each other so profoundly.

While many women are called to make a gift of themselves through physical motherhood, it is the calling of every woman to make a gift of herself through spiritual motherhood. Spiritual motherhood means coming alongside and investing in the lives of younger women, through formation, wisdom, support, and encouragement. This is true for the single woman, the woman who is unable to have her own children, and the woman who is celibate.

This task cannot be underestimated. It is vital for all women to be spiritually mothering and mentoring the women who walk with them. In some cultures, older women can feel as if they no longer have anything to offer. This is a great poverty, as they in fact have a whole lifetime of wisdom desperately needed by all women, and indeed the whole world.

In seeking to build a civilization of love, it is essential that as women we begin a journey of discovering the genius of womanhood. It is only then that we will truly be all that God intended us to be.

The vocation of every woman is for motherhood: this can take the form of spiritual and physical motherhood.

Spiritual motherhood is the calling of every woman.

"[V]irginity has to be considered *also as a path for women*, a path on which they realize their womanhood in a way different from marriage."[7]

John Paul II

"Whether lived out or remaining potential, this capacity (for new life) is a reality that structures the female personality in a profound way." [5]

John Paul II

Little princesses grow up to be bigger princesses... so show them the way.

"The mother is filled with wonder at this mystery of life, and 'understands' with unique intuition what is happening inside her.

In the light of the 'beginning,' the mother accepts and loves as a person the child she is carrying in her womb. This unique contact with the new human being developing within her gives rise to an attitude towards human beings—not only towards her own child,

but every human being—which profoundly marks the woman's personality." [9]

John Paul II

So many **women** today feel that they are a problem. If only they knew the profound truth of their existence...

...That they are in fact an **answer** to so many of society's problems.

It depends on women to promote a
new feminism, one that rejects the imitation
of men and one that seeks equality not from
a position of power but rather from a position of
love...not just a human love but more
profoundly a divine love.

This new feminism must be based on a deep **reflection** on the very nature and design of **woman** herself.

"It is thus my hope, dear sisters, that you will reflect carefully on what it means to speak of the 'genius of women,' not only in order to be able to see in this phrase a specific part of God's plan which needs to be accepted and appreciated, but also in order to let this genius be more fully expressed in the life of society as a whole, as well as in the life of the Church."[10]

John Paul II

Notes

1. Karol Wojtyla, *Love and Responsibility* (San Francisco: Ignatius Press, 1981), 55.

2. John Paul II, *Evangelium Vitae: The Gospel of Life* (Boston: Pauline Books & Media, 1995), no. 99.

3. John Paul II, *Mulieris Dignitatem: On the Dignity and Vocation of Women* (Boston: Pauline Books & Media, 1999), no. 29.

4. *Mulieris Dignitatem*, no. 25.

5. Ibid, no. 10.

6. The Council's *Message to Women* (Dec. 8, 1965); The Holy See, http://www.vatican.va/holy_father/paul_vi/speeches/1965/documents/hf_p-vi_spe_19651208_epilogo-concilio-donne_en.html.

7. *Mulieris Dignitatem*, no. 20.

8. John Paul II, *Letter to the Bishops of the Catholic Church on the Collaboration of Men and Women in the Church and in the World*, no. 13, The Holy See, http://www.vatican.va/roman_curia/congregations/cfaith/documents/rc_con_cfaith_doc_20040731_collaboration_en.html.

9. *Mulieris Dignitatem*, no. 18.

10. John Paul II, *Letter of Pope John Paul II to Women* (Boston: Pauline Books & Media, 1998) no. 10.

Also Available

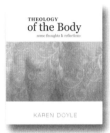

Theology of the Body

Some Thoughts and Reflections

Karen Doyle

Some basic reflections on key ideas of Pope John Paul II's ground-breaking work, the Theology of the Body. By returning to "the beginning," and examining God's plan for life and love prior to original sin, we see that, through the redeeming love of Jesus Christ, true and lasting happiness and fulfillment are possible in our lives and relationships.

0-8198-7427-2 $10.95

Other books on the Theology of the Body

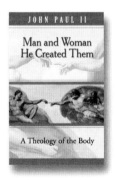

Man and Woman He Created Them

John Paul II

A new translation of the complete text of John Paul II's monumental work, which he himself called "theology of the body." Includes a comprehensive introduction, translator's footnotes, and a detailed index.

0-8198-7421-3 $29.95

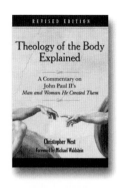

Theology of the Body Explained
A Commentary on John Paul II's
Man and Woman He Created Them

Christopher West

Unpacks the entire work of the theology of the body. Revised and expanded to reflect the improved translation and new scholarship.

0-8198-7425-6 $29.95

The Theology of the Body Made Simple

Anthony Percy

A simple introduction to the theology of the body.

0-8198-7419-1 $9.95

God's Plan for You
Life, Love, Marriage, and Sex

David Hajduk

John Paul II's theology of the body made accessible for teens, answering their questions about life, relationships, and sexuality.

0-8198-4517-5 $16.95

Order at www.pauline.org, or by calling
Pauline Books & Media at 1-800-876-4463,
or through the book and media center nearest you.

Pauline
BOOKS & MEDIA

A mission of the Daughters of St. Paul

As apostles of Jesus Christ, evangelizing today's world:

We are CALLED to holiness
by God's living Word and Eucharist.

We COMMUNICATE the Gospel message
through our lives and through all
available forms of media.

We SERVE the Church
by responding to the hopes and needs
of all people with the Word of God,
in the spirit of St. Paul.

For more information visit our website: www.pauline.org.

auline
BOOKS & MEDIA

The Daughters of St. Paul operate book and media centers at the following addresses. Visit, call or write the one nearest you today, or find us on the World Wide Web, www.pauline.org

CALIFORNIA
3908 Sepulveda Blvd, Culver City, CA 90230	310-397-8676
2640 Broadway Street, Redwood City, CA 94063	650-369-4230
5945 Balboa Avenue, San Diego, CA 92111	858-565-9181

FLORIDA
145 S.W. 107th Avenue, Miami, FL 33174	305-559-6715

HAWAII
1143 Bishop Street, Honolulu, HI 96813	808-521-2731
Neighbor Islands call:	866-521-2731

ILLINOIS
172 North Michigan Avenue, Chicago, IL 60601	312-346-4228

LOUISIANA
4403 Veterans Memorial Blvd, Metairie, LA 70006	504-887-7631

MASSACHUSETTS
885 Providence Hwy, Dedham, MA 02026	781-326-5385

MISSOURI
9804 Watson Road, St. Louis, MO 63126	314-965-3512

NEW JERSEY
561 U.S. Route 1, Wick Plaza, Edison, NJ 08817	732-572-1200

NEW YORK
64 W. 38th Street, New York, NY 10018	212-754-1110

PENNSYLVANIA
9171-A Roosevelt Blvd, Philadelphia, PA 19114	215-676-9494

SOUTH CAROLINA
243 King Street, Charleston, SC 29401	843-577-0175

VIRGINIA
1025 King Street, Alexandria, VA 22314	703-549-3806

CANADA
3022 Dufferin Street, Toronto, ON M6B 3T5	416-781-9131

¡También somos su fuente para libros,
videos y música en español!